Umbrellas

Umbrellas

Judith Pinkerton Josephson

Carolrhoda Books, Inc./Minneapolis

The photographs in this book are reproduced through the courtesy of: Hollywood Book & Poster, cover (top middle), pp. 37 (bottom), 38 (both), 42; IPS, cover (top right, bottom right, middle left), pp. 2, 3, 5, 6 (top), 8 (both), 10, 17 (right), 18, 23 (bottom), 26 (bottom), 29 (left), 30 (bottom), 31 (bottom), 32 (both), 34 (bottom), 39 (bottom), 41, 43 (bottom); Corbis-Bettmann, cover (bottom left), pp. 11 (right), 15 (both), 19, 20, 21, 22, 24, 27 (top), 36, 40 (bottom); UPI/Corbis-Bettmann, pp. 1, 11 (left), 13 (bottom), 29 (right), 30 (top); © Mike Magnuson, p. 6 (bottom); © Howard E. Ande, p. 7; John Erste, pp. 9, 44-45; © Photograph by Erich Lessing, Art Resource, p. 12; Archive Photos, pp. 13 (top), 14 (top); Mansell/ Time Inc., p. 14; l'Osservatore Romano, Città del Vaticano, Servizio Fotografico/ CNS, p. 16; © Museum of London, p. 17 (left); Archive Photos/Ed Grazda, p. 23 (top); The Goldstein: A Museum of Design, University of Minnesota, pp. 25 (left), 27 (bottom), 28; Bob Croxford/Atmosphere Postcards, Cornwall, U.K., p. 25 (right); © Museum of Costume and Textiles, Nottingham, UK, p. 26 (top); Morton International, p. 31 (top); Totes Inc., p. 33 (bottom); © Sean Sprague, Panos Pictures, p. 33 (top); Christine Osborne Pictures/ Maghreb Press Agency/MEP, p. 34 (top); © 1991 Star Paul, staff photo by John Croft, p. 35; Lambert/Archive Photos, p. 37 (top); The Bridgeman Art Library International Ltd., p. 39 (right); Reuters/Kimimasa Mayama/ Archive Photos, p. 40 (top); Illustration from "Piglet Is Entirely Surrounded by Water" from Winnie-the-Pooh by A. A. Milne, illustrated by E. H. Shepard. Copyright 1926 by E. P. Dutton, renewed 1954 by A. A. Milne. Used by permission of Dutton Children's Books, a division of Penguin Books USA Inc., p. 42 (top); AP Photo/ Katsumi Kasahara, p. 43 (top); © 1993 Jason Laure, p. 46; Reuters/Will Burgess/ Archive Photos, p. 47.

To Ron, Kirsten, and Erika, with love

Thanks to Edith Fine, Jill Hansen, Suzan Wilson, Melissa Irick, Kitty Morse, Mary Pinkerton, and my wonderful Encinitas Writers' Group, for reading and listening to the manuscript and offering suggestions. Thanks also to my editors, Jill Anderson and Gwenyth Swain, for believing in the idea and helping me mold the manuscript into proper umbrella shape.

An excerpt from SINGIN' IN THE RAIN by Nacio Herb Brown and Arthur Freed © 1929 (renewed), Metro-Goldwyn-Mayer Inc., appears on page 38. All rights controlled by EMI Robbins Catalog Inc., WARNER BROS. PUBLICATIONS U.S. INC., Miami, FL, 33014.

Words that appear in **bold** in the text are listed in the glossary on page 46.

Text copyright © 1998 by Judith Pinkerton Josephson.

Carolrhoda Books, Inc. c/o The Lerner Publishing Group
241 First Avenue North, Minneapolis, MN 55401 U.S.A.
Website address: www.lernerbooks.com

Library of Congress Cataloging-in-Publication Data

Josephson, Judith Pinkerton.
  Umbrellas / by Judith Pinkerton Josephson.
    p. cm.
  Includes index.
  Summary: Presents the history of umbrellas and includes an explanation of how they work, how they came to be, and how their purpose and popularity have changed over time.
  ISBN 1-57505-098-6
  1. Umbrellas and parasols—Social aspects—Juvenile literature.
2. Umbrellas and parasols—History—Juvenile literature. [1. Umbrellas and parasols.]
GT2210.U43 1998
391.4'4—dc21   97-23988

Manufactured in the United States of America
1 2 3 4 5 6 - JR - 03 02 01 00 99 98

Contents

Umbrellas dot the sidewalks on rainy days.

Rain, Rain, Go Away

Splish! Splash! Plink! Plunk! Rain dances on the sidewalk. Rustle, swish, pop! Colorful **umbrellas** sprout like mushrooms.

All over the world, umbrellas are as common as raindrops. On wet days, students open small **collapsible umbrellas.** Young children splash through puddles, twirling umbrellas decorated with jungle creatures, polka dots, and cartoon characters. On sunny days, beachgoers duck under large umbrellas propped in the sand. On hot afternoons, people sip lemonade under red-and-white striped patio umbrellas.

Some parts of the globe are rainier than others, and umbrellas come in handy in these soggy spots. The wettest place on earth is on top of a volcano on the big island of Hawaii. There, 451 inches of rain fall each year. Deep in the rain forest near the Amazon River in Brazil, it rains almost 100 inches a year. Countries like Sri Lanka are wet *and* hot. People there use umbrellas to keep out both rain and sun.

Made in the Shade

The word *umbrella* comes from *umbra,* the Latin word for "shade" or "shadow." **Parasol,** another name for an umbrella, means "to guard against the sun." Even though *umbrella* and *parasol* once meant the same thing, neither term had anything to do with rain. Although umbrellas appeared more than three thousand years ago, they didn't become popular for rain until the 1700s. Think how wet everybody got before then! Ever since the objects began to sprout up in foul weather, *umbrella* has more often described rain gear, while *parasol* means strictly a sunshade.

The first umbrellas were little more than bowls balanced upside-down on sticks. Modern umbrellas are stronger and better at keeping us dry.

Umbrellas help people beat the heat and sun on a Chicago, Illinois, beach.

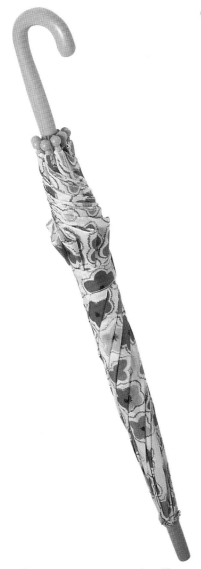

Open up your umbrella and take a look at the frame inside.

They are made of lighter, waterproof fabrics and factory-made parts. Still, the umbrella's basic shape and structure have stayed the same.

How an Umbrella Works

The best way to understand how an umbrella works is to open one up and take a peek underneath. At the center of the umbrella is the long straight **shaft** that holds the umbrella up. At the bottom of the shaft is the handle. Handles can be curved or straight. Most shafts and handles are made of wood, steel, or plastic.

At the top of the umbrella shaft are eight to ten **ribs.** Strong and flexible, they are usually made of aluminum, steel, or hard plastic. The ribs form a curved frame for the **cover,** the keep-you-dry part of an umbrella. Most modern umbrella covers are made from tough, waterproof nylon or polyester. Attached to the middle of each rib is a thin metal piece called a **stretcher.** The stretchers help stretch the fabric and attach to the **runner,** a short tube around the shaft. The runner slides up and down between two **springs** at the top and bottom of the shaft.

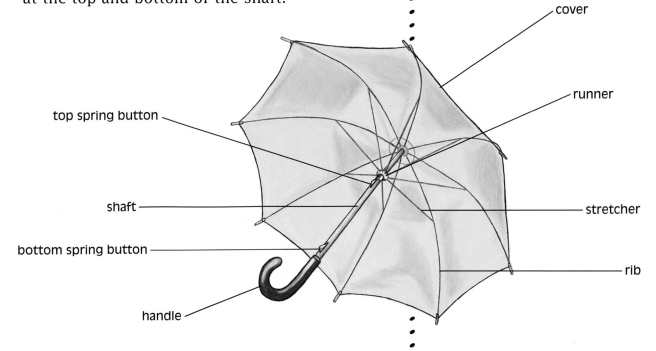

cover

runner

top spring button

shaft

bottom spring button

handle

stretcher

rib

Umbrella Care

Here's how to take care of an umbrella:

1. Carefully unfasten the strap from around the umbrella.
2. Unroll the cover.
3. Gently slide the runner up the shaft until it clicks into place.
4. Always let your umbrella cover dry before rolling it up again.
5. Don't twist the ribs when you roll the cover around the shaft.
6. Put your name and phone number on your umbrella in case you leave it somewhere.

The runner and stretchers do most of the work of an umbrella. As the runner and stretchers slide up the shaft . . . Presto! The umbrella pops open, the cover stretches tightly over the ribs, and the top spring clicks. To close the umbrella, you press a button to release the spring and pull the runner toward you as the runner slides down the shaft. That action pulls in the ribs and folds up the umbrella. A narrow strap with a snap, button, or sticky Velcro strip wraps tightly around the cover to keep the umbrella closed.

Take good care of your umbrella, and it will last a long time.

Umbrellas usually work well—but watch out for those big gusts of wind!

All these parts usually work smoothly together, except during a big storm. One strong gust and POOF! Your umbrella may turn into a jumble of spokes and crumpled cloth. You'll run for cover just as people did long ago.

The king of Assyria rides under an elaborate umbrella in this scene carved in stone in the 700s B.C.

Sunshine, Sultans, & Showing Off

The world's first umbrellas popped up sometime around 1300 B.C. People in Egypt, India, and China carried umbrellas as a shade from the sun. Kings, queens, and emperors used huge, showy umbrellas to impress people with royal power and might.

In its earliest days, the umbrella was also a religious symbol. The ancient Egyptians believed that the goddess Nut sheltered the earth like an umbrella. Her arched body, tummy side down, formed the big bowl of the sky. Only the goddess's toes and fingertips touched the earth.

Left: The Egyptian goddess Nut
Below: State umbrellas are still used. King Norodom Sihanouk of Cambodia stands under an umbrella made of tin in 1941.

A god named Shu held Nut's body in the air, just the way the shaft and ribs support a real umbrella. Stars on the goddess's belly twinkled in the night sky. The Egyptians thought that people who walked under umbrellas would have the goddess Nut's heavenly protection.

Fit For a King (or Queen)

Royal umbrella owners liked the attention that a fancy model brought the person underneath. The more umbrellas a king owned, the more important he seemed. The bigger and fancier they were, the better! These umbrellas were called **state umbrellas,** and they were more for show than for shade.

In Ethiopia important leaders walk under colorful umbrellas.

In Italy in the 1200s, the artist who made this mosaic indicated royalty by putting an umbrella over the king and queen.

Some state umbrellas stood fifteen feet high—as tall as a giraffe—and were heavy enough to make a strong man stagger. Important people never had to carry their own umbrellas. Servants or slaves did that. One Chinese emperor wasn't even satisfied to go about with a single, grand umbrella. He required a parade of a dozen, and that was on just an ordinary day! Just in case people copied the custom, some rulers passed laws making it a crime to carry an umbrella unless you were a king or queen. (That made staying out of the sun difficult for common people.)

Carrying umbrellas gradually became acceptable for upper-class folks in other parts of the world, but at first only for women. In China, Japan, and other Asian countries, parasol covers were made from silk, cotton, or rice paper, and decorated with flowers, butterflies, and other beautiful designs. The covers were coated with oil or varnish, a shiny liquid that dries to form a protective coating. These Asian parasols shaded the face but were too fragile to be of much use in a downpour.

In about 500 B.C., umbrella fashion spread to ancient Greece. There, upper-class women carried small white parasols to protect their skin from the bright sun. Women of lower classes had to find other means of protection, as did men. The only excuse a Greek man could use for carrying a parasol was that he was holding it over a woman.

Parasols with ribs and shafts made of bamboo became popular in Asian countries.

Left: A young woman stands under an umbrella in this painting on a Greek vase from about 440 B.C.

Church leaders continue to use umbrellas for important events—and to stay dry. Pope John Paul II (above) keeps out of the rain under a large white umbrella. At one time, aides carried the pope on their shoulders in a special chair called the *sedia gestatoria*. An umbrella-like canopy above the chair shielded the pope from the sun.

Of Heavenly Importance

Church leaders copied kings, emperors, and other rulers. In Italy in the 1400s, the leader of the Catholic church, the pope, appeared under a red and yellow silk umbrella called the papilionus (pa-puh-lee-OH-nus). His assistants, cardinals and bishops, had umbrellas of violet or green. Soon, Catholic churches adopted the umbrella as a symbol of heavenly protection and the power of the church. Because umbrellas often gave importance to special occasions and ceremonies, they were called **ceremonial umbrellas.**

A few centuries later, in some Protestant churches, huge umbrellas were held over ministers at burial services or when going to visit the sick. These ministers realized that, besides adding importance to ceremonies, umbrellas made staying dry during a rain shower a snap. Although no common folk would think of carrying such a funny-looking contraption just to stay dry, nobody dared to make fun of a minister.

Using an umbrella in the rain didn't catch on right away, but the idea kept spreading. By the 1600s in Italy, both men and women used umbrellas as sunshades. Many were made of leather stretched over a round wooden frame.

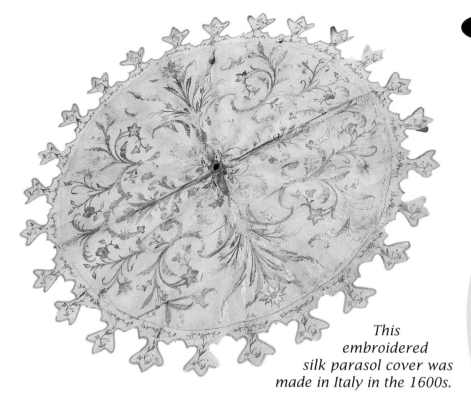

This embroidered silk parasol cover was made in Italy in the 1600s.

These days most people use sunscreen lotion and a hat to protect themselves from the sun. And not many people use umbrellas and parasols just for show, either. But wouldn't it be fun, just once, to have a dozen umbrellas announce *your* arrival at school, at a movie or play, or a championship game? As your umbrella parade passed by, people might say, "Wow! That person must be really important!"

At traditional Jewish wedding ceremonies, the bride and groom stand under an umbrella-like canopy called a *huppah*. The canopy (above) is a symbol for the roof of a couple's new home.

In Africa an Ashanti bride traditionally walked to the home of her new husband under an umbrella. It was meant to shield the newlyweds from harm so that they would have good crops and many children.

Like this umbrella from the mid-1900s, many early rain umbrellas had cotton covers. Once these umbrellas became soaked, rain dripped on the wearer's head.

Bumbershoots and Brollies

It took a long time for people to decide that umbrellas were useful for both rain and sun. The first signs of acceptance appeared two thousand years ago in ancient Rome. Women began to carry oiled parasols to chariot races and other sporting events. When it started to drizzle—PHOOSH!—hundreds of parasols popped open. Men sitting nearby complained that the umbrellas blocked their view. The Roman emperor ruled that the women had the right to protect themselves from getting wet. Even so, these rain shields soon dropped out of sight. It took an umbrella pioneer named Jonas Hanway to make umbrellas a common sight on a rainy day.

The Umbrella Man

In Jonas Hanway's travels to countries such as Italy and Portugal, the young English business-man had seen umbrellas used not just for sun but sometimes in rain and snow too. Coming from a country famous for its drizzly weather, Hanway thought this was a great idea. In those days, many men wore their hair curled, pow-dered, and tied at the back of the neck. Rain showers made a mess of their hairdos. Hanway also believed the umbrella might keep him from catching cold. Around 1750, he brought an um-brella home with him and carried it whenever it rained (some say even when it was sunny).

Jonas Hanway was an important man who had given money to charities. Yet people laughed at him. Children chased and teased him. They thought Hanway (and anyone who copied him) looked silly and girlish carrying an umbrella. Why on earth would a man carry a tent over his head when all he had to do was put on a hat?

Although most Londoners thought he looked funny, Jonas Hanway knew his umbrella kept him and his powdered wig dry.

Opposite page: A man models the latest fashion in umbrellas in 1820. Below: Some alternatives to umbrellas, such as this English hood, were just plain odd.

Coachmen feared Hanway would put them out of business. These men held giant **carriage umbrellas** over people as they dashed between their carriages and the doors to coffee houses or shops. If people started carrying their own umbrellas, no one would need a coachman. So, to make Hanway look bad, coachmen purposely drove their carriages through puddles to spatter mud on him. Hanway ignored them and lugged his umbrella wherever he went.

Just Plain Odd

Nobody—not even Jonas Hanway—really knew how to carry an umbrella without looking silly. Early models were big and clunky, with ribs and shafts made of heavy cane or whalebone. Some were so heavy they had to be rested upon the shoulder. Worse yet, the covers leaked!

At first those English people who did use umbrellas carried them only for short, wet walks or at rainy funerals. Other people continued to dash about in a downpour as they always had, wearing overcoats and broad-brimmed hats or throwing shawls or capes over their heads. Parasols hadn't caught on for sunny weather in England, either.

Across the ocean in the British colonies (which became the United States in 1776), it took even longer for people to accept umbrellas and parasols as useful. Colonial women usually carried giant fans or wore bonnets, kerchiefs, or caps to protect their faces from the sun. When a Connecticut woman first used an umbrella imported from the West Indies, she shocked her neighbors. They made fun of her by prancing around carrying kitchen strainers balanced on broomsticks.

In the southern colonies, in the steaming heat of summer, more people were tempted by the cooling shade of parasols. Slowly women began to accept umbrellas for both sun and rain. But people still laughed at men who took shelter under umbrellas. Umbrellas were just plain odd, people said—certainly not for hardy colonists.

A Jolly Good Idea!

Little by little, people on both sides of the Atlantic changed their minds. By 1800 both men and women agreed that umbrellas came in handy. During a storm, peole preferred arriving somewhere dry instead of staggering in soaking wet. Buying an umbrella was cheaper than hiring a horse and carriage whenever it rained.

Early umbrella users were superstitious. They believed that tying an acorn to the base of the handle would protect them from being struck by lightning. Some people still consider it bad luck to open an umbrella indoors, to give an umbrella as a gift, or to place an umbrella on a bed or table.

A parade of umbrella users leaves a London umbrella shop in the 1830s.

Umbrellas made good sunshades, walking sticks, shields, and even weapons. With the sharp tip of a closed umbrella, a person could fight off a wild bull, a mad dog, or a robber. For a while, the British called umbrellas "Hanways" after their biggest fan. Eventually, they became known as "brollies."

A crowd of people in Vietnam wear umbrella-shaped hats.

Sometimes an umbrella can also be a hat.

Broad-brimmed hats can work just like umbrellas to protect the wearer from the weather. Some people in Asian countries, especially farmers, have long worn cone-shaped hats as sunshades. The hat's shape is similar to that of parasols from the region, without the handle.

People had the same idea in countries like Mexico, where the sun shines most of the year. Sombreros have brims as wide as small umbrellas.

In the United States, inventors have combined the shelter of an umbrella with the convenience of a hat. Look, Ma, no hands!

Right: A black umbrella was an important part of a gentleman's outfit in the late 1800s.
Opposite page, left: A satin umbrella from the 1800s

As ideas about umbrellas gradually changed, business picked up for umbrella makers in England and other places. The number of shops that made and sold umbrellas increased. By 1851 there were 1,330 workers in the industry in London alone. Following over a hundred small steps, workers made the ribs, shafts, covers, and handles. Other workers hand-stitched the covers or attached the covers to the frames.

Customers now had many different cover materials to choose from, including silk, cotton, oilcloth, and wax-glazed linen. One glossy cotton fabric was named after the French town of Guingamp. Because of this, some people nicknamed the umbrella the "gamp."

Writer Charles Dickens even named one of his characters Mrs. Sarah Gamp in his story, *The Life and Adventures of Martin Chuzzlewit.* Mrs. Gamp carried an untidy, battered umbrella that she sometimes jabbed at other people. Americans called the umbrella "bumbershoot" because of its similarity to the parachute, invented in 1779.

In the 1800s, one person was so excited about umbrellas that he built a cottage in the shape of one. The umbrella cottage stood high on a hill in Lyme Regis, Dorset, England. The thatched roof was trimmed to look just like an umbrella cover. A chimney poked through the middle of the roof, just like the tip of a real umbrella.

Of the improved steel rib, Samuel Fox & Co. said, "... Nothing equal to it has ever yet been brought out."

Inventors scrambled to create new and better designs. In 1840 Henry Holland was one of several inventors who tried making ribs out of tubes of steel, which were much lighter than whalebone. Samuel Fox improved on Holland's ideas. By 1847 Fox had a patent and began to sell his improved steel umbrella ribs.

A new profession grew out of the umbrella's popularity. When the wind twisted umbrellas into inside-out messes, someone had to fix them. People who repaired them often did their work right in their customers' homes. In London a red umbrella posted outside a shop announced that broken umbrellas were mended there.

This umbrella has many sturdy steel ribs.

Feathers, Frills, and Fashion

As umbrellas for rain became more common, so did lightweight fashion parasols for women. Just like fans, muffs, and gloves, parasols became part of women's outfits. Many parasols were made of silk, satin, velvet, or lace. Trimmings included lace, fringe, gold and silver braid, ribbons, bows, feathers, and glass trinkets. Fancy handles were carved from ivory, onyx, or wood. During the 1800s, couples often spent sunny afternoons strolling in the park. Waving in the wind, ladies' elegant parasols looked like colorful flowers. The frilly accessory also had a practical side: it shaded the skin.

A frilly lace parasol

Most women's parasols were flimsy, but Victoria, queen of England from 1837 to 1901, had a better idea. After someone tried to kill her, she had one of her parasols lined with the same chain mail, or iron mesh, that knights wore under their armor to protect their bodies.

Some parasols tilted for better sun protection and folded for easy carrying.

In the 1800s in Belgium, where one word for *umbrella* is "parapluie," a dance called *la parapluiterie* was popular. A woman holding an umbrella had to choose between two dance partners. She gave the umbrella to the man she did *not* want to dance with. That unlucky man had to hold the umbrella over the couple while they danced.

Around 1830 parasols even became part of a lively French dance called the cancan. Performers balanced lacy parasols on their shoulders and tossed their ruffly skirts back and forth. As they kicked their legs high in the air, both their petticoats and their legs showed—a very daring thing to do during this prim and proper time.

Since parasols were all about looking good, styles changed along with fashion. In the mid-1800s, many women wore **bustles,** pads that rested on the backside but were hidden beneath the skirts of their dresses. Bustles made dresses pouf out in back. A new style of parasol appeared that was wide enough to shade the whole dress, bustle and all.

Men followed fashion too. Around 1860 a new type of hat called a **derby** came into fashion in England. Made of felt, derbies were easily ruined by rain. The stylish solution was the **rolled umbrella.** The cover of a rolled umbrella, almost always black, wrapped tightly around the shaft when closed. Soon no well-dressed gentleman would stroll the rainy London streets without his brolly. When the sun peeked out from behind the clouds, WHOOSH! Down went the brolly. Tightly rolled, it became a jaunty walking stick.

Left: Where do you put an umbrella when it's not being used? This antique umbrella stand is one answer.
Right: A proper Englishman with his brolly

Attending car races in France in 1922, these women carry fancy en-tout-cas *umbrellas to protect them from rain and sun.*

An early waterproof umbrella

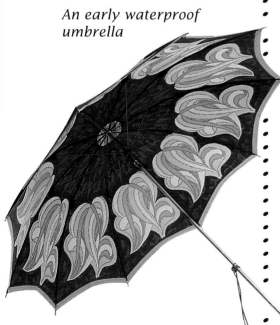

Toward the end of the 1800s, women began to enjoy biking, hiking, and other outdoor activities. This more active lifestyle led to a cross between an umbrella and a parasol called an **en-tout-cas** (ahn-too-KAH), popular in England and France. More brightly colored than an umbrella but larger and plainer than a parasol, the *en-tout-cas* worked in both sunny and rainy weather. (The word means "in all cases" in French.) Umbrellas and parasols continued to be popular into the early 1900s.

Modern Umbrellas

Modern umbrellas come in hundreds of sizes, colors, and patterns. You name it—stars and moons, watermelons, even a picture of Elvis Presley—it's on an umbrella somewhere. Some umbrellas even have designs on the *underside* of the cover. Sheltered from the raindrops, you can look up at a famous painting or puffy clouds in a bright blue sky.

Until the early 1900s, cooking salt would clump and get stuck in the salt shaker whenever the weather was rainy. In 1913 Morton Salt introduced a new and improved salt that didn't clump. The Morton Salt Girl, holding a big umbrella, was (and still is) pictured on the label along with the slogan "When it rains, it pours."

Some umbrellas give you pictures to look at from underneath.

Above: In the mid-1900s, nylon, polyester, and plastic became popular materials for umbrella covers.
Right: Collapsible umbrellas

Nylon, invented in 1938, and later, polyester and plastic have replaced the cotton and silk traditionally used for covers. No more leaks! Although some umbrella shafts are still made of wood or steel, plastic and fiberglass are also popular. One umbrella maker, the English Umbrella Company, makes its stretchers and ribs out of tempered carbon steel. The company boasts that these parts are so strong and flexible that the umbrella can turn inside out and nothing breaks!

In the 1960s, a new type of umbrella hit the market: the collapsible umbrella. When closed, the lower half of the shaft fits inside the upper half, and the ribs tuck into a hollow handle.

Sometimes as short as six inches, these umbrellas fit easily into backpacks, briefcases, and large purses. And when it rains, you can pop them open with one hand and the click of a button.

Most modern umbrellas are made in factories. Machines sew covers and do other jobs that people once did by hand. Engineers have found better ways to attach covers to shafts and stretchers to ribs and runners. It also takes less time to make an umbrella than it did when they were made by hand. This has made umbrellas much more affordable.

Above: In Thailand a worker makes umbrellas by hand.
Left: Even factory-made umbrellas require some handwork.

James Smith & Sons of London, England, has been selling umbrellas since 1830.

From department stores to grocery and hardware stores, umbrellas are for sale in all sorts of places—sometimes for as little as $10. Only a few of the old umbrella shops remain. These shops make fine, hand-finished umbrellas that sell for $50 to $800. One of the oldest of these shops is James Smith & Sons, in London. It carries hundreds of umbrellas, most with nylon covers. Some of the shop's umbrellas have handles made of bamboo, ivory, silver, maple, or buffalo horn. The shop even has state and ceremonial umbrellas, and umbrellas that turn into seats. No wonder princes stop by! The shop sells five hundred umbrellas each month and repairs at least two thousand.

Umbrella handles come in all shapes and sizes.

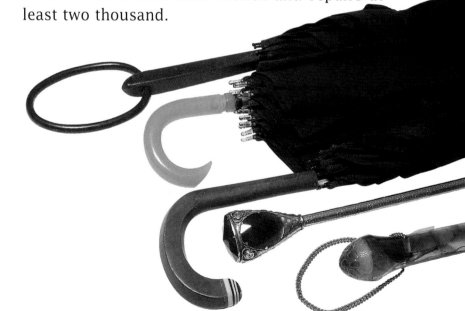

At an American football game, fans huddle under umbrellas.

Many folks nowadays own several umbrellas, and for good reason! Every year thousands of umbrellas are left behind on trains, buses, and planes, and in schools, restaurants, and shops. Do you have a name tag on yours? If you do, you and your forgotten umbrella have a better chance of finding each other again. Otherwise, when feather-soft raindrops drizzle and drum, you'll get as wet as the weather!

The umbrellabird lives in the tropical forests of Central and South America. About the size of a crow, the bird lives in the tops of the highest trees. The male has an umbrella-shaped crest on the top of his head. A flap below his neck looks like an umbrella handle. To show off for his mate, the umbrellabird raises and fluffs out his glossy blue-black feathers.

Nobody wants to have a broken umbrella on a rainy day.

Singin' in the Rain

If Jonas Hanway were alive, he would feel proud. Umbrellas are everywhere, especially when it rains. With new proof that sun can hurt the skin, people all over the world are still using the umbrella as a sunshade too.

The English have honored Hanway by naming a street and lane in the heart of London after him. A Jonas Hanway monument in Westminster Abbey praises him for having raised money for hospitals and orphanages. It also mentions one of his favorite sayings, "Never despair!" Hanway followed his own advice. He didn't give up until he had convinced people that umbrellas were useful objects.

Let a Smile Be Your Umbrella

Umbrellas still make people laugh, but not for the same reasons people laughed at Jonas Hanway. When a gust of wind turns an umbrella inside out, the person carrying it grabs for the handle and struggles to hold on. People watching may get the giggles—until the wind does the same thing to their umbrellas.

Umbrellas also get laughs at the circus. A clown with orange hair and a red nose rides a tricycle into the ring. He honks his horn. Sirens wail. Whistles blow. Over his head, the clown holds a ridiculously small umbrella. The crowd laughs and cheers.

Umbrellas can be good for a laugh (left) or for keeping dry (below).

In the movie *Mary Poppins,* Mary, the new nanny, arrives at the Banks home looking very dignified—except that she floats down out of the clouds with the help of a black umbrella. Mary's umbrella even sports a talking parrot for a handle!

One of the most memorable moments in movie history appeared in the 1952 film *Singin' in the Rain.* Holding an umbrella, actor Gene Kelly dances up and down the street, on and off the curb. As he splashes through puddles in the pouring rain, he sings: "Just singin' in the rain, singin' in the rain. What a glorious feeling, I'm happy again. . . . " At the end of the scene, Kelly hands his umbrella to a surprised passerby and walks off in the rain.

The Art of the Umbrella

Because umbrellas are so popular, many artists have included them in their paintings. In *A Sunday Afternoon on the Island of La Grande Jatte*, painted by French impressionist Georges Seurat in the late 1800s, families stroll and read books under umbrellas in the park on a sunny afternoon. In *The Umbrellas,* by Pierre-Auguste Renoir, a rainy day turns a crowded street into a sea of blue-black umbrellas. You can buy a copy of one famous umbrella painting, *Paris Street: Rainy Day,* by Gustave Caillebotte, printed on the cover of an umbrella.

Above: Renoir's The Umbrellas
Left: Caillebotte's Paris Street: Rainy Day *covers an umbrella.*

Right: Christo's umbrellas tower over Japanese schoolchildren.

Let a tree be your umbrella? This umbrella-shaped tree was grown at a botanical garden.

Another artist, Christo, likes to think big. In a 1991 display called *The Umbrellas,* he linked Japan and the United States by cranking open 3,100 gigantic umbrellas in the two countries on the same day. Each umbrella was almost 20 feet tall, 28 feet wide, and weighed about 485 pounds. You and 50 friends could fit under an umbrella that big!

Millions of people flocked to see Christo's umbrellas. In the mountains north of Los Angeles, California, 1,760 yellow umbrellas created a "golden forest." At the same time, near Tokyo, Japan, 1,340 blue umbrellas became a giant garden, blue as cornflowers. The two sites together covered 75 miles. The artist called the massive umbrellas his "children."

Umbrellas to the Rescue

An umbrella saved the day for make-believe explorer Robinson Crusoe. In the novel *Robinson Crusoe,* written by Daniel Defoe in 1719, Crusoe washes ashore on a deserted South Seas island. He soon realizes that he needs something to protect himself from the blazing sun. Crusoe remembers umbrellas he had seen in Brazil and sets out to build one. After several tries, he manages to make an umbrella out of animal hides, with the fur side up. The umbrella even goes up and down. Crusoe and his umbrella were so popular with readers that umbrellas were once called "Robinsons" in France.

Robinson Crusoe takes a walk with his dog and his umbrella.

Umbrella Names

Chinese: yu shan
French: parapluie
German: Regenschirm
Italian: ombrello
Japanese: higasa
Spanish: paraguas (for rain);
    parasol (for sun)
Swedish: paraply

Christopher Robin helps Winnie-the-Pooh stay afloat during a rainstorm.

Jiminy Cricket appeared with his umbrella in the Disney movie Pinocchio.

In the much-loved book *Winnie-the-Pooh,* by A. A. Milne, Christopher Robin and Pooh Bear stage a daring rescue with an umbrella. Piglet gets trapped in a tree and "surrounded by water" during a rainstorm. His two friends turn an umbrella upside down to make a wobbly boat. To Piglet's joy, they save him from the "Terrible Flood."

Here to Stay

Three thousand years after it first appeared, the umbrella keeps popping up. At various times in history, the umbrella has been a sunshade, a fancy fashion item, a walking stick, and a symbol of rank, power, and wealth. Museums in England, Italy, and elsewhere have collections of umbrellas and parasols. There's even a name for the study of umbrellas—"brolliology." Our modern world is filled with hair dryers, dishwashers, can openers, and millions of other gadgets. Yet, when the white-hot sun shines or when it's raining cats and dogs, people reach for a simple solution—the umbrella.

CRACKLE, SIZZLE, BOOM, CRASH!
SPRINKLE, DRIP, DROP, POUR!
Now, where *did* I put my umbrella?

This Japanese woman gives her shoes extra protection from sun and rain by wearing special shoe umbrellas.

You Will Need:

for the cookies

1 roll of ready-made sugar
cookie dough

cookie sheet

cooking spray

table knife

spatula

frosting (see ingredients on
page 45)

A Rainy-Day Treat

*Next time you're stuck inside on a rainy day, invite
some friends over to make umbrella-shaped cookies.*

1. Put cookie dough in freezer for 15 to 30 minutes,
   until firm but not hard. Ask an adult to preheat
   oven to 350 degrees Fahrenheit. Spray cookie
   sheet with cooking spray and set aside.

2. Using a table knife, cut 8 to 10 thin (1/4-inch)
   slices of dough. If slices aren't round, gently re-
   shape them. Put several circles aside and cut the
   rest in half. Place half circles 3 inches apart on
   cookie sheet. These are your umbrella covers.
   When cookie sheet is full, wrap uncut dough and
   return to freezer.

3. From circles of dough set aside, cut thin (1/4-inch-wide) strips for umbrella shafts. Place one end of each strip in the middle of the straight side of a half circle and press lightly to mold the pieces together. Shape shafts any way you wish.

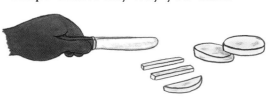

4. Ask an adult to help you bake cookies for 6 to 8 minutes or until the edges turn golden. Using an oven mitt, remove from oven and let cool on cookie sheet. Carefully remove cookies from sheet with a spatula and cool completely. Take remaining dough from freezer and repeat steps 1 through 4 until dough is gone.

5. To make frosting, stir together in a small bowl sifted powdered sugar, milk, and vanilla until smooth. Add more milk if frosting is too thick, or more sugar if frosting is too thin. Divide frosting among several small bowls and add a different color of food coloring to each. Stir well. Use table knives, spoons, or toothpicks to spread frosting on cookies. To finish decorating, be creative! Thin strips of licorice can make colorful umbrella ribs. Sprinkles can be raindrops. Red hots can make polka dots.

You Will Need:

for the frosting

small bowls

1 cup powdered sugar, sifted

3 tablespoons milk

1/2 teaspoon vanilla

food coloring

table knives, spoons, toothpicks

sprinkles, licorice, red hots (optional)

In Capetown, South Africa, men parade with colorful umbrellas during a local festival.

Glossary

bustles: pads worn under dresses to make the skirts flow out over the wearers' backsides

carriage umbrellas: large umbrellas used by coachmen to shield groups of people as they dashed from their carriages to stores, homes, or other buildings

ceremonial umbrella: an umbrella, usually highly decorated, that is used in a religious ceremony or service

collapsible umbrellas: umbrellas that fold and shorten for easier carrying

cover: the cloth or plastic that stretches over the umbrella frame to protect the carrier from rain or sun

derby: a small, rounded felt hat fashionable in the 1800s and worn by British men

en-tout-cas: a stylish umbrella used as both a sunshade and a rain shield

parasol: an umbrella used as a sunshade and often as a fashion accessory

ribs: the strong, flexible strips of metal, wood, or plastic that hold the fabric of the umbrella in place

rolled umbrella: an umbrella that rolls up tightly when closed and sometimes doubles as a walking stick

runner: the round tube that slides up and down to open and close an umbrella

shaft: the stick in the center of the umbrella

springs: wire coils at the top and bottom of an umbrella stick that hold the runner in either a closed or an open position

state umbrellas: fancy umbrellas used by government leaders to make them look important

stretcher: a thin metal piece that connects each rib to the runner

umbrella: an object made of fabric or plastic stretched tightly over a frame. Held over the head, an umbrella protects the user from rain and sometimes from sun.

Below: A canopy of red umbrellas covers a walkway during spring festival celebrations in Beijing, China.

Index